# CONTENTS



Words in the glossary appear in **bold** type the first time they are used in the text.

# WINDOW TO THE PAST

Have you ever written or received a letter? Today, letters are a less common form of **communication**. But, in the past, letters were the only kind of communication! We can use letters as primary sources to learn about people and the past.

A LOOK AT PRIMARY SOURCES

# LETTERS

BY KRISTEN RAJCZAK NELSON

Gareth Stevens Publishing

CRASHCOURSE

Please visit our website, www.garethstevens.com. For a free color catalog of all our high-quality books, call toll free 1-800-542-2595 or fax 1-877-542-2596.

**Library of Congress Cataloging-in-Publication Data**

Names: Rajczak Nelson, Kristen, author.
Title: Letters / Kristen Rajczak Nelson.
Description: Buffalo, New York : Gareth Stevens Publishing, 2024. | Series: A look at primary sources | Includes index.
Identifiers: LCCN 2022056606 (print) | LCCN 2022056607 (ebook) | ISBN 9781538287507 (hardcover) | ISBN 9781538287491 (paperback) | ISBN 9781538287514 (ebook)
Subjects: LCSH: History--Sources--Juvenile literature. | Letters--Juvenile literature. | Biography--Juvenile literature. | Historiography--Juvenile literature.
Classification: LCC D16.14 .R354 2024 (print) | LCC D16.14 (ebook) | DDC 907.2--dc23/eng/20230110
LC record available at https://lccn.loc.gov/2022056606
LC ebook record available at https://lccn.loc.gov/2022056607

First Edition

Published in 2024 by
Gareth Stevens Publishing
2544 Clinton Street
Buffalo, NY 14224



Designer: Claire Wrazin
Editor: Kristen Rajczak Nelson

Photo credits: Cover (photo), pp. 11, 15, 17, 27 Courtesy of Library of Congress; series art (background texture) Verbena/Shutterstock.com; series art (cover typeface) Gleb Guralnyk/Shutterstock.com; p. 5 Scisetti Alfio/Shutterstock.com; p. 7 File:NYTimes-Page1-11-11-1918.jpg/Wikimedia Commons; p. 7 (photos) Volodymyr Nikitenko/Shutterstock.con; pp. 9, 13 (woman) fizkes/Shutterstock.com; series art (photo frame) Nataliia K/Shutterstock.com; pp. 13 (man), 23 Rawpixel.com/Shutterstock.com; p. 19 (letter) File:HandschriftJohnAdams.jpg/Wikimedia Commons; p. 19 (envelopes) Militarist/Shutterstock.com; p. 21 LiliGraphie/Shutterstock.com; p. 23 View Apart/Shutterstock.com; p. 25 Everett Collection/Shutterstock.com; p. 29 NicoElNino/Shutterstock.com.



Printed in the United States of America

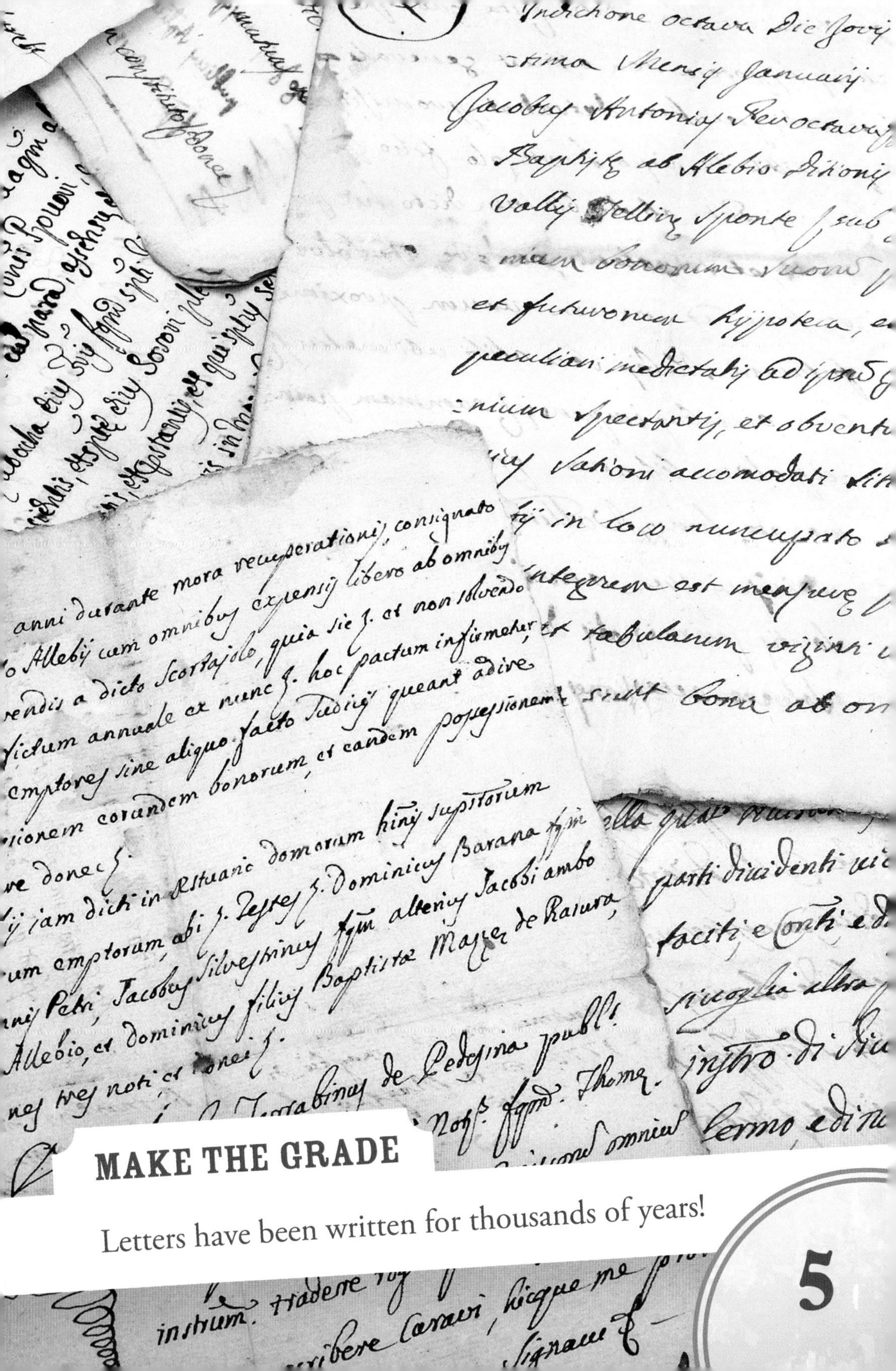

## MAKE THE GRADE

Letters have been written for thousands of years!

# FROM THE SOURCE

A primary source is an account of something that happened from a person who was there. It can be a newspaper, a photograph, or a piece of art made about the event, or happening.

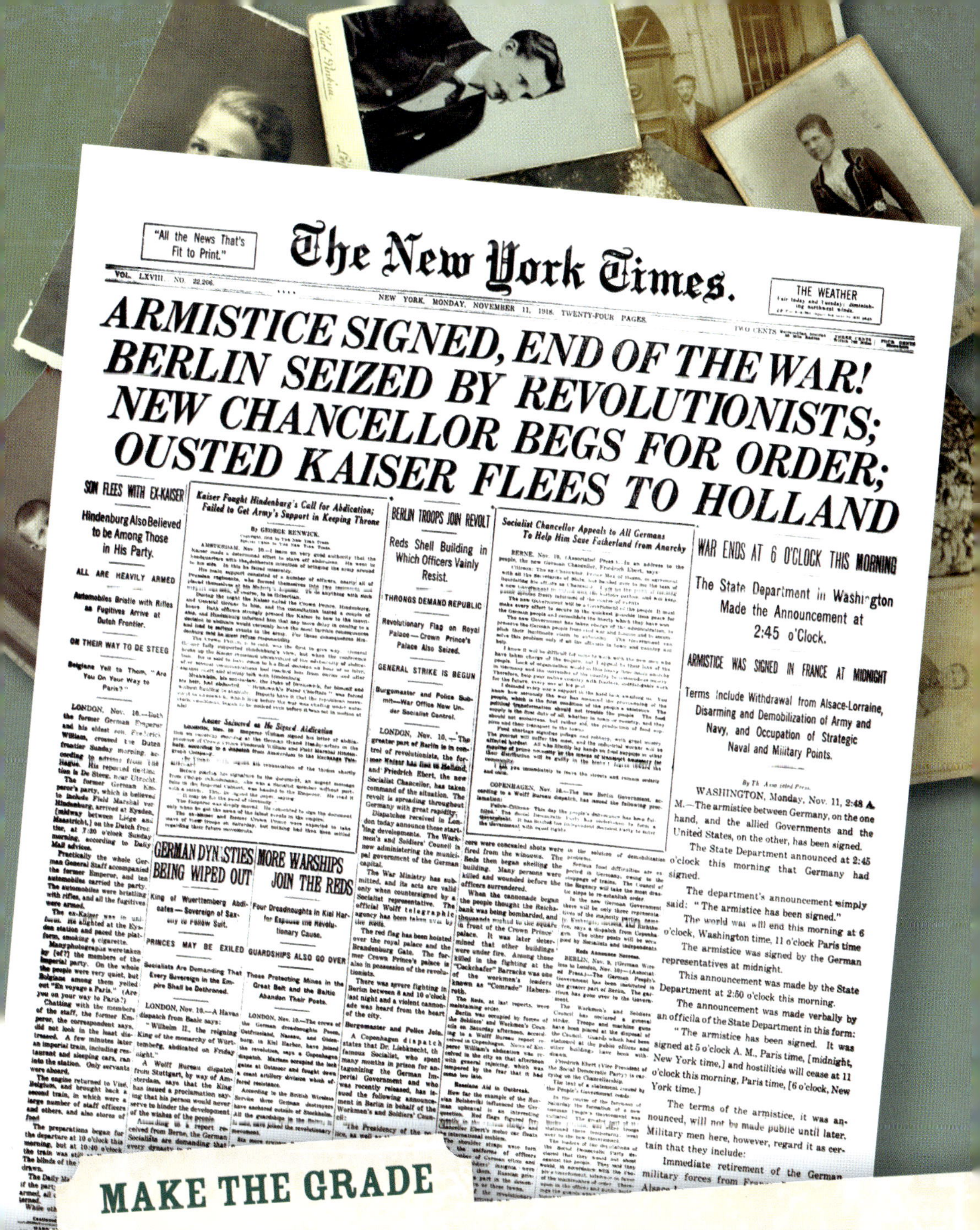

"All the News That's Fit to Print."

The New York Times.

VOL. LXVIII...NO. 22,266. NEW YORK, MONDAY, NOVEMBER 11, 1918. TWENTY-FOUR PAGES.

THE WEATHER

# ARMISTICE SIGNED, END OF THE WAR! BERLIN SEIZED BY REVOLUTIONISTS; NEW CHANCELLOR BEGS FOR ORDER; OUSTED KAISER FLEES TO HOLLAND

SON FLEES WITH EX-KAISER

Hindenburg Also Believed to be Among Those in His Party.

ALL ARE HEAVILY ARMED

Automobiles Bristle with Rifles as Fugitives Arrive at Dutch Frontier.

ON THEIR WAY TO DE STEEG

Kaiser Fought Hindenburg's Call for Abdication; Failed to Get Army's Support in Keeping Throne

BERLIN TROOPS JOIN REVOLT

Reds Shell Building in Which Officers Vainly Resist.

THRONGS DEMAND REPUBLIC

Revolutionary Flag on Royal Palace—Crown Prince's Palace Also Seized.

GENERAL STRIKE IS BEGUN

Socialist Chancellor Appeals to All Germans To Help Him Save Fatherland from Anarchy

GERMAN DYNASTIES BEING WIPED OUT

MORE WARSHIPS JOIN THE REDS

WAR ENDS AT 6 O'CLOCK THIS MORNING

The State Department in Washington Made the Announcement at 2:45 o'Clock.

ARMISTICE WAS SIGNED IN FRANCE AT MIDNIGHT

Terms Include Withdrawal from Alsace-Lorraine, Disarming and Demobilization of Army and Navy, and Occupation of Strategic Naval and Military Points.

WASHINGTON, Monday, Nov. 11, 2:48 A. M.—The armistice between Germany, on the one hand, and the allied Governments and the United States, on the other, has been signed.

The State Department announced at 2:45 o'clock this morning that Germany had signed.

The department's announcement simply said: "The armistice has been signed."

The world war will end this morning at 6 o'clock, Washington time, 11 o'clock Paris time.

The armistice was signed by the German representatives at midnight.

This announcement was made by the State Department at 2:50 o'clock this morning.

The announcement was made verbally by an officia of the State Department in this form:

"The armistice has been signed. It was signed at 5 o'clock A. M., Paris time, [midnight, New York time,] and hostilities will cease at 11 o'clock this morning, Paris time, [6 o'clock, New York time.]

The terms of the armistice, it was announced, will not be made public until later. Military men here, however, regard it as certain that they include:

Immediate retirement of the German military forces from France...

## MAKE THE GRADE

Letters can be secondary sources too. These are sources that comment on a primary source or **interpret** it.

# ABOUT LETTERS

There are a few kinds of letters. Friendly letters are those written in an **informal** way. They may be to friends or family. They tell about daily life and events. Business letters are more **formal**.

### MAKE THE GRADE

Business letters can be between a person and a company, two people in business together, or used for other formal matters.

All letters have some of the same features. The greeting often gives the name of who the letter is to. The ending and signature, or signed name, tell who the letter is from. Many letters from history have a date too, giving the time period it's from.

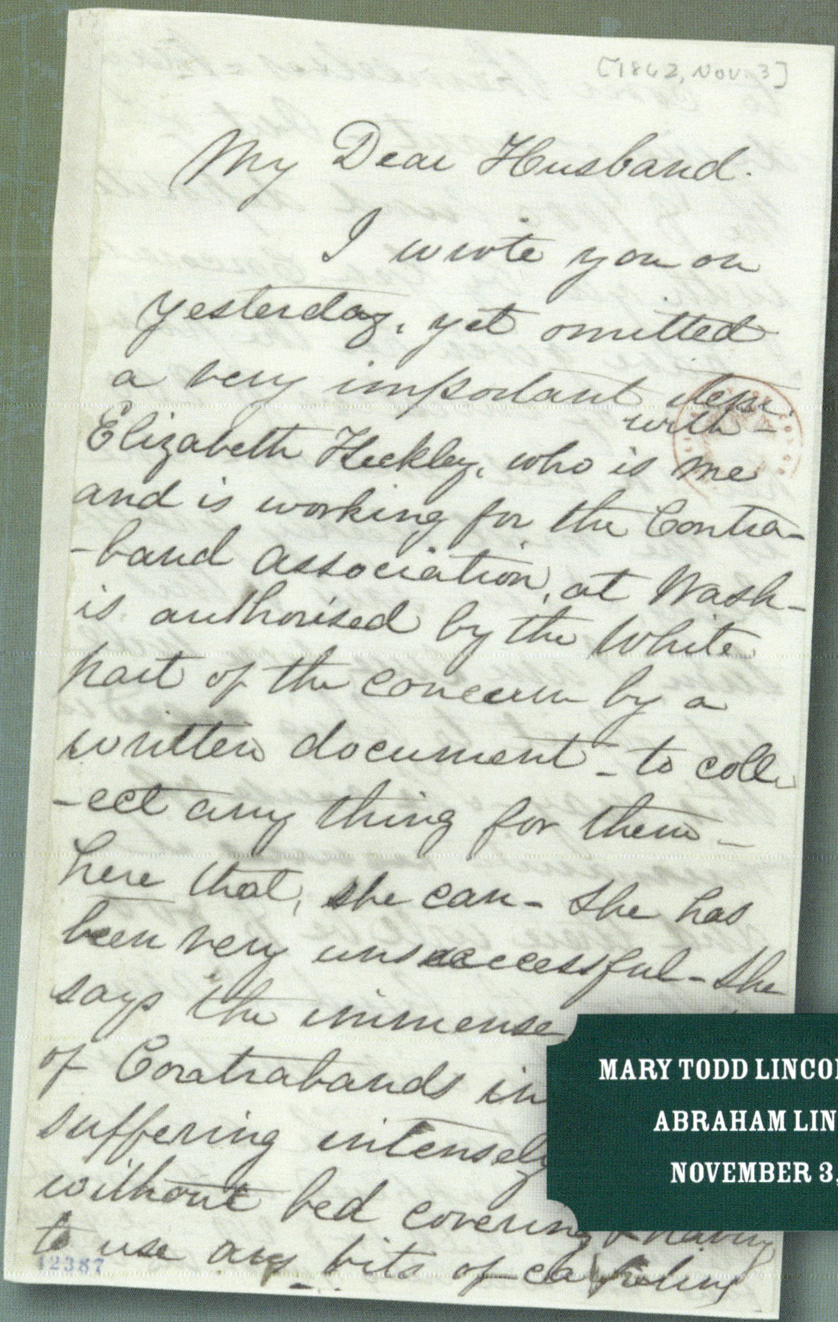
[1862, Nov 3]

My Dear Husband.

I wrote you on
yesterday, yet omitted
a very important item.
Elizabeth Keckley, who is with me
and is working for the Contra-
-band association, at Wash-
is authorised by the White
part of the concern by a
written document - to coll-
-ect any thing for them -
here that, she can - She has
been very unsuccessful - She
says the immense
of Contrabands in
suffering intensely
without bed covering [illegible]
to use any bits of clothing

MARY TODD LINCOLN TO ABRAHAM LINCOLN NOVEMBER 3, 1862

## MAKE THE GRADE

Some letters include addresses. This lets us know where the letter was going to or coming from.

# ONE SIDE

When using letters as primary sources, it's important to remember a letter is one part of a dialogue. In order to know the whole story, you may need the letter's reply! Or, you may need the letter your source was replying to.

## MAKE THE GRADE

A dialogue is a communication—written or in-person—between two or more people.

# COLLECTING LETTERS

Many times, letters written by historical figures are collected. The collection will often also include letters written to the person. They may give a whole written dialogue. It takes many years to collect letters that may have been sent all over the world!

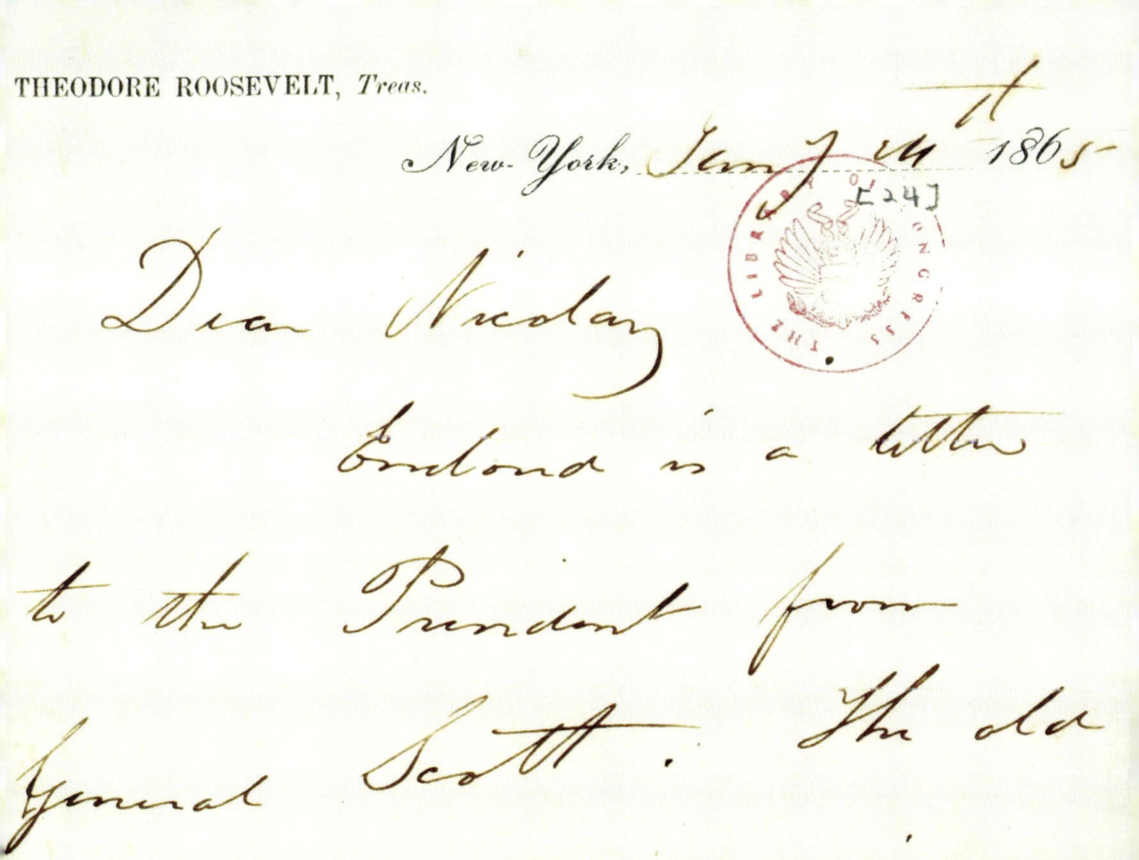

THEODORE ROOSEVELT, *Treas.*

New-York, Jany 24th 1865

Dear Nicolay

Enclosed is a letter to the President from General Scott. The old General is very much interested in the Association

THEODORE ROOSEVELT TO JOHN G. NICOLAY, JANUARY 24, 1865

## MAKE THE GRADE

The letters of U.S. presidents, such as Theodore Roosevelt, are often collected by places that show old items, like museums, as well as colleges and libraries.

# LOOKING INTO HISTORY

Letters are great primary sources for historical **research**. They can teach about the time period they are from. A letter could include the **politics** of the day. It may discuss what's happening in an area during a war.

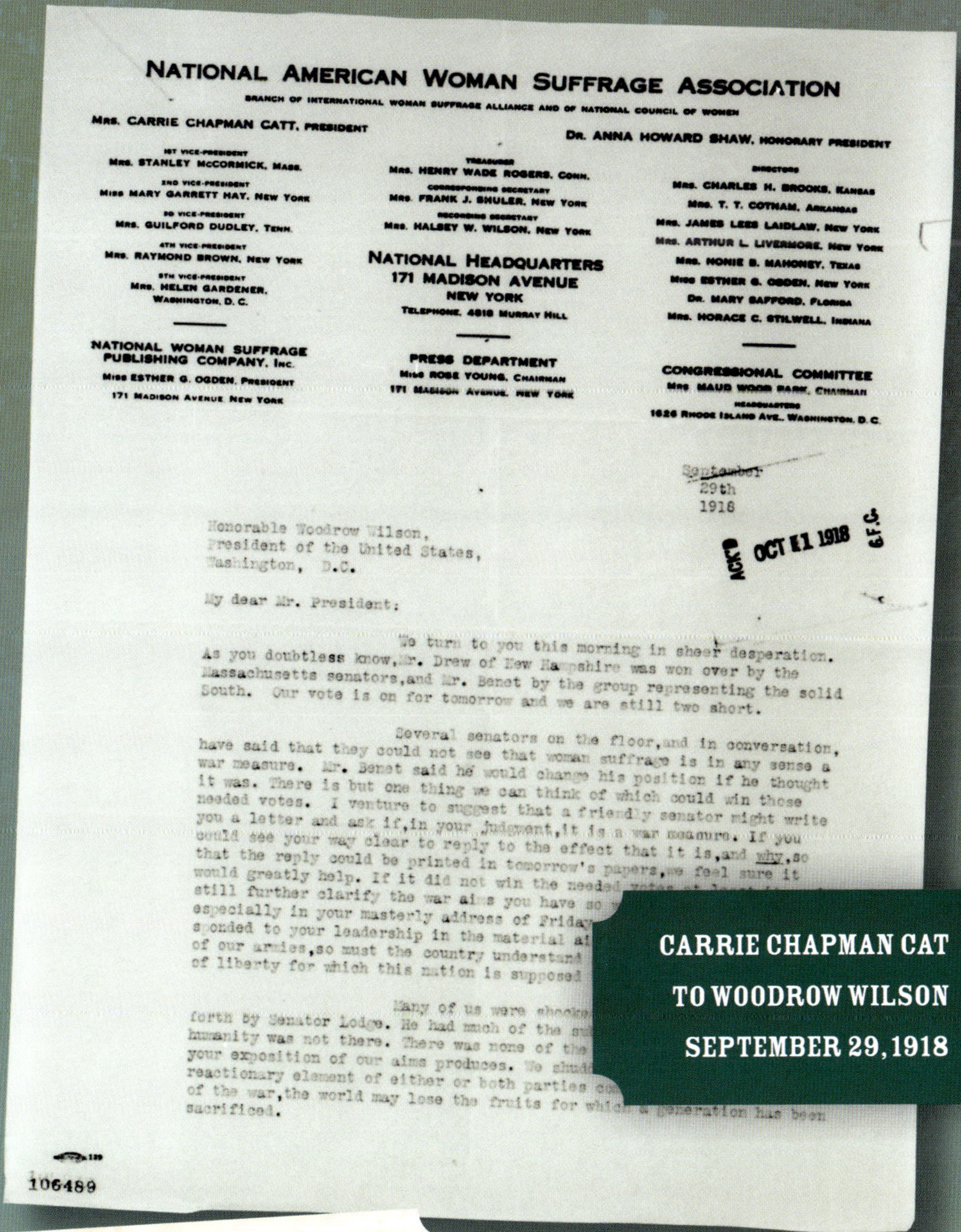

NATIONAL AMERICAN WOMAN SUFFRAGE ASSOCIATION

BRANCH OF INTERNATIONAL WOMAN SUFFRAGE ALLIANCE AND OF NATIONAL COUNCIL OF WOMEN

MRS. CARRIE CHAPMAN CATT, PRESIDENT

DR. ANNA HOWARD SHAW, HONORARY PRESIDENT

1ST VICE-PRESIDENT
MRS. STANLEY McCORMICK, MASS.
2ND VICE-PRESIDENT
MISS MARY GARRETT HAY, NEW YORK
3D VICE-PRESIDENT
MRS. GUILFORD DUDLEY, TENN.
4TH VICE-PRESIDENT
MRS. RAYMOND BROWN, NEW YORK
5TH VICE-PRESIDENT
MRS. HELEN GARDENER, WASHINGTON, D. C.

NATIONAL WOMAN SUFFRAGE PUBLISHING COMPANY, INC.
MISS ESTHER G. OGDEN, PRESIDENT
171 MADISON AVENUE NEW YORK

TREASURER
MRS. HENRY WADE ROGERS, CONN.
CORRESPONDING SECRETARY
MRS. FRANK J. SHULER, NEW YORK
RECORDING SECRETARY
MRS. HALSEY W. WILSON, NEW YORK

NATIONAL HEADQUARTERS
171 MADISON AVENUE
NEW YORK
TELEPHONE, 4818 MURRAY HILL

PRESS DEPARTMENT
MISS ROSE YOUNG, CHAIRMAN
171 MADISON AVENUE, NEW YORK

DIRECTORS
MRS. CHARLES H. BROOKS, KANSAS
MRS. T. T. COTNAM, ARKANSAS
MRS. JAMES LEES LAIDLAW, NEW YORK
MRS. ARTHUR L. LIVERMORE, NEW YORK
MRS. NONIE B. MAHONEY, TEXAS
MISS ESTHER G. OGDEN, NEW YORK
DR. MARY SAFFORD, FLORIDA
MRS. HORACE C. STILWELL, INDIANA

CONGRESSIONAL COMMITTEE
MRS MAUD WOOD PARK, CHAIRMAN
HEADQUARTERS
1626 RHODE ISLAND AVE., WASHINGTON, D. C.

~~September~~
29th
1918

ACK'D OCT 1 1918 G.F.C.

Honorable Woodrow Wilson,
President of the United States,
Washington, D.C.

My dear Mr. President:

We turn to you this morning in sheer desperation. As you doubtless know, Mr. Drew of New Hampshire was won over by the Massachusetts senators, and Mr. Benet by the group representing the solid South. Our vote is on for tomorrow and we are still two short.

Several senators on the floor, and in conversation, have said that they could not see that woman suffrage is in any sense a war measure. Mr. Benet said he would change his position if he thought it was. There is but one thing we can think of which could win those needed votes. I venture to suggest that a friendly senator might write you a letter and ask if, in your judgment, it is a war measure. If you could see your way clear to reply to the effect that it is, and <u>why</u>, so that the reply could be printed in tomorrow's papers, we feel sure it would greatly help. If it did not win the needed
still further clarify the war aims you have so
especially in your masterly address of Friday
sponded to your leadership in the material ai
of our armies, so must the country understand
of liberty for which this nation is supposed

Many of us were shocke
forth by Senator Lodge. He had much of the su
humanity was not there. There was none of the
your exposition of our aims produces. We shudd
reactionary element of either or both parties co
of the war, the world may lose the fruits for which a generation has been sacrificed.

106489

CARRIE CHAPMAN CAT
TO WOODROW WILSON
SEPTEMBER 29, 1918

## MAKE THE GRADE

Letters offer a view of a culture at a certain time in history. Culture includes the beliefs and ways of life of a group of people.

Letters are often used as a primary source for research about a person. Historians may read the person's **correspondence** in order to learn more about their **relationships**. Letters often have personal thoughts and facts in them not found anywhere else.

Amsterdam Septr. 15. 1780

My dear Portia.

I wish you to write me by every opportunity to this Place, as well as to France. — It seems as if I never should get any more Letters from America. I have sent you some Things by Captn. Davis, but he has no Arms, and I fear they will be lost, by Capture. — I sent Things by the Alliance.

The Country where I am is the greatest Curiosity in the World. — This Nation is not known, any where not even by its Neighbours. — The Dutch Language is Spoken by none but themselves. — Therefore They converse with no body and no body converses with them. — The English are a great nation, and they despise the Dutch because they are smaller. — The French are a greater Nation still, and therefore they despise the Dutch because they are still smaller in comparison to them.

But I doubt much whether there is any Nation of Europe more estimable than the Dutch, in Proportion.

JOHN ADAMS TO ABIGAIL ADAMS
SEPTEMBER 15, 1780

## MAKE THE GRADE

John and Abigail Adams wrote many letters. From these, historians have learned how important she was to his thinking during his presidency.

Common people are given a voice through their letters. Letters from people who went West by wagon train in the 1800s offer a look at what those journeys were like. Letters home from soldiers show what life was like for those on the battlefield.

## MAKE THE GRADE

For much of history, mail wasn't **reliable**. Sometimes, people would write many letters before receiving one reply!

A person's point of view is how they look at or think about something. All letters are written from one person's point of view. They may include **biases**. Some of these beliefs may be seen as incorrect or unacceptable today.

## MAKE THE GRADE

Exploring letters from history allows us to see how the world has changed, including ideas about how the government should be run.

# COLLABORATION THROUGH CORRESPONDENCE

Scientists have used correspondence to talk about their ideas. Charles Darwin wrote many letters. He used them for research and **debate**. His letters show not only his thoughts, but also how scientists work together.

CHARLES DARWIN

## MAKE THE GRADE

Charles Darwin is famous for his theories, or scientific ideas, of evolution. Evolution includes the ways living things have slowly changed over time.

# ORIGINAL, COPY, OR ONLINE

Today, historical letters are carefully taken care of. Copies can be seen in books. They may be viewed in online collections. Even though you aren't seeing the original letter, it's still a primary source! What's written in it hasn't changed.

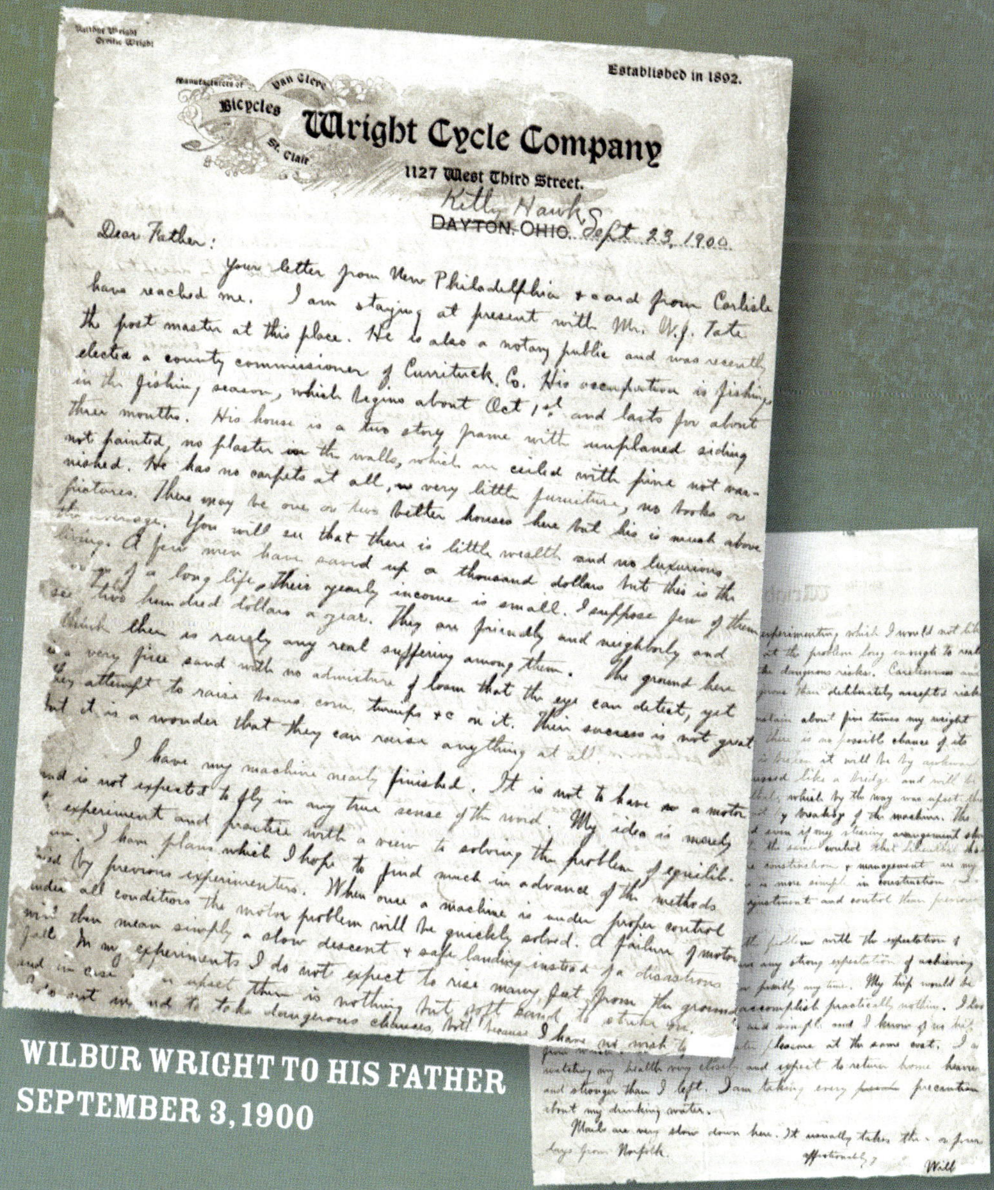

Wilbur Wright
Orville Wright

Established in 1892.

Manufacturers of Van Cleve Bicycles St. Clair

Wright Cycle Company

1127 West Third Street.

~~DAYTON, OHIO~~ Kitty Hawk, Sept 23, 1900

Dear Father:

Your letter from New Philadelphia & card from Carlisle have reached me. I am staying at present with Mr. W. J. Tate the post master at this place. He is also a notary public and was recently elected a county commissioner of Currituck Co. His occupation is fishing in the fishing season, which begins about Oct 1st and lasts for about three months. His house is a two story frame with unplaned siding not painted, no plaster on the walls, which are ceiled with pine not varnished. He has no carpets at all, very little furniture, no books or pictures. There may be one or two better houses here but his is much above the average. You will see that there is little wealth and no luxurious living. A few men have saved up a thousand dollars but this is the result of a long life. Their yearly income is small. I suppose few of them see two hundred dollars a year. They are friendly and neighborly and I think there is rarely any real suffering among them. The ground here is a very fine sand with no admixture of loam that the eye can detect, yet they attempt to raise beans, corn, turnips &c on it. Their success is not great but it is a wonder that they can raise anything at all.

I have my machine nearly finished. It is not to have a motor and is not expected to fly in any true sense of the word. My idea is merely to experiment and practice with a view to solving the problem of equilibrium. I have plans which I hope to find much in advance of the methods tried by previous experimenters. When once a machine is under proper control under all conditions the motor problem will be quickly solved. A failure of motor will then mean simply a slow descent & safe landing instead of a disastrous fall. In my experiments I do not expect to rise many feet from the ground and in case ... upset there is nothing but soft sand to strike on. I do not intend to take dangerous chances, both because I have not wish ...

... watching my health very closely and expect to return home heavier and stronger than I left. I am taking every possible precaution about my drinking water.

Mails are very slow down here. It usually takes three or four days from Norfolk.

Affectionately,
Will

WILBUR WRIGHT TO HIS FATHER
SEPTEMBER 3, 1900

## MAKE THE GRADE

The U.S. Library of Congress has a large online collection of letters. These include some written by the men who flew the first powered flight, Wilbur and Orville Wright.

# MODERN LETTERS

Most letters today are sent electronically! Like letters, emails can be used as primary sources. One day, historians may be checking your emails to see what you thought of the world around you!

## MAKE THE GRADE

The first email was sent in 1971.

# USING LETTERS AS A PRIMARY SOURCE

**Visit the Library of Congress website to find a letter from history (*www.loc.gov/collections/*) or ask a teacher, caregiver, or grandparent if they have any old letters you can read.**

**Read the letter.** *What does it say?*

**Look at the letter.** Find the greeting and closing to learn who it is to and from. Check for a date and any addresses. You can use the Library of Congress information to help with this.

**When you know the date when it was written, consider the following questions:**

- *What can this letter tell you about that time?*
- *Were any events discussed?*
- *What is the relationship between the writer and the person receiving the letter?*
- *What thoughts did the writer express that are different from your own?*

**Look up other sources that can help you better understand your letter.** You can use a newspaper from the same time, photographs, or books. *Did the new source change what you think about the letter?*

# GLOSSARY

**bias:** To have an unfair preference or dislike of something.

**communication:** Sharing thoughts or feelings by sound, movement, or writing.

**correspondence:** The letters or emails sent between people.

**debate:** To argue a side.

**formal:** Following an established form. Also, having a tone of respect.

**informal:** Not formal or relaxed.

**interpret:** To explain the meaning of something.

**politics:** The activities of the government and government officials.

**relationship:** A connection to another person.

**reliable:** Able to do what is needed.

**research:** Studying to find something new.

# FOR MORE INFORMATION

## BOOKS

Boswell, Kelly. *Research Primary Source Documents: Diaries, Letters, Journals, and More!*. North Mankato, MN: Pebble, 2019.

Brooks, Ben. *Dare to Be Different: Inspirational Words from People Who Changed the World.* Philadelphia, PA: RP Kids, 2022.

## WEBSITES

**Primary vs. Secondary**
*umb.libguides.com/PrimarySources/secondary*
Compare primary and secondary sources, and find examples of each, on this website.



# INDEX